D1304371

101
QUESTIONS
ABOUT
SANTA
CLAUS

Accurately Recorded
by Bob Litak

BLUE SKY MARKETING INC.
PO Box 21583-S St. Paul, MN 55121 USA

101 Questions About Santa Claus

Copyright © 1998 by Robert E. Litak
Just B. Claus Productions
PO Box 902, Cedarburg, WI 53012
Fax (414) 377-4800
All rights reserved.

Design by Roth Creative Services
Edited by Christine Hilt Muehlenberg

Printed in the United States of America
ISBN: 0-911493-23-9

Published In North America by:
BLUE SKY MARKETING INC.
PO Box 21583-S
St. Paul, MN 55121 USA
(651) 456-5602 / 800-444-5450
SAN 263-9394

8   7   6   5

Dedicated to
Mrs. Claus,
The Elves, Christmas Sherry,
and
All of My "Helpers"

Foreword

Okay, right now you're asking yourself,
"How does this guy know all about Santa Claus?"

Well, to tell the truth, I don't know *all* about
Santa Claus. But I do know a bit more than most
people. Most importantly, I speak from first-hand
experience!

For twelve years I was as close to Santa as
anyone could be. *(In fact, you might have had some
trouble telling us apart. Many people did.)* I had the
distinct privilege to work with Mrs. Claus, the Elves,
the Reindeer, a whole host of his North Pole friends,
and a large number of his dedicated "Helpers." What
I'm telling you is absolutely true, and if you care to
check it out, you can *(but that's another story altogether).*

I won't promise you that this book will provide
the answers to everything you want to know about
Santa. But I can assure you that within its pages
you'll find out some things you didn't know as well as
some truly surprising Santa facts.

So, if you've ever wondered about Santa, had to
explain something about him to another, or been the
least bit curious about the truths of the myth, read
on, my friend.

When you're finished, you'll be able to answer
that most important Santa question of all.

Bob Litak

-1-
How do Santa's Reindeer fly?

This question's the one most frequently asked of Santa. The amazing answer is that they don't!

Santa's Reindeer, like their generic cousins, are mammals. They have neither wings nor feathers, and even if they did, their body structure makes them far too heavy for flight. What they do possess are unusually strong hind legs and a unique type of aerodynamically shaped antlers.

By carefully adjusting the angle of their antlers to the strength of their leap, Santa's Reindeer are able to remain airborne for distances of several feet to several thousand miles.

For years, those fortunate enough to have observed Santa's Reindeer during one of their "lengthy leaps," have mistakenly reported them "flying." You're welcome to continue to speak of them as flying, but now, you know the truth.

$$V = \frac{R^8 + R\,[A \times O \times A]}{S^1 + S^2 + T^1}\,(12 \times 25)$$

-2-
How fast do Santa's Reindeer go?

Santa and his Reindeer travel at speeds impossible to measure by current scientific instruments. They can accelerate from a "rooftop stop" to faster than the speed of light in the twinkling of an eye.

For those who are scientifically inclined, and have a working knowledge of Yuletide physics, the formula at the top of the page will provide a simple method for determining their maximum speed.

For those of us not quite so technically gifted, the equation translates to: **V** (velocity/speed) equals **R^8** (Reindeer, to the eighth power) plus **R** (Rudolph), multiplied by **AOA** (angle of antlers), divided by **S^1** (Santa), plus **S^2** (sleigh), plus **T^1** (toys), which is multiplied by **12** (December) and again by **25** (Christmas Day).

-3-
How did the Reindeer get their names?

Actually, they named each other.

Dancer named Prancer;
Prancer named Vixen;
Vixen named Blitzen;
Blitzen named Cupid;
Cupid named Donner;
Donner named Comet;
Comet named Dasher;
and Dasher named Dancer.

Rudolph, who was the last to join the team,
arrived already named.

How old is Santa Claus?

Santa admits to being several hundred years old. However, he neither cares nor finds it necessary to remember exactly how old he is. All he needs to know is that each year he is reborn in the hearts of those who harbor the love and warmth of the Christmas spirit. He's not sure if this rebirth makes him one year older or one year younger.

As long as you believe in him, he will exist forever.

-5-
How old is Mrs. Claus?

Mrs. Claus is one year younger than Santa.

-6-
Does Mrs. Claus have a first name?

Yes, she does. It's Anne.

Does Mrs. Claus have a "Nick" name for Santa?

As a matter of fact, she does.

Mrs. Claus affectionately calls Santa J.O.E.*

Jolly Old Elf!

-8-
Why does Santa live at the North Pole?

There are several reasons.

First, the remoteness of the North Pole assures Santa, Mrs. Claus, the Elves, and the Reindeer of the peace, quiet, and seclusion needed to carry on their important and time-consuming tasks.

With the exception of an occasional explorer or soda-peddling polar bear, centuries may pass without a knock at the door.

Second, the position of the North Pole, at the very top of the world, makes it an ideal location from which to observe the behavior of all of the little boys and girls of the world.

Third, had Santa decided to reside at the South Pole,

the print in this book would be upside down!

-9-

How does Santa understand all the different languages of the world's children?

As the world's most senior Senior Citizen, and the universally recognized ambassador to all the world's children, Santa is able to read and speak every language known to humankind.

He's also capable of speaking to most animals *(and is particularly fluent in Reindeer),* and can converse in all of the 9,999,999 dialects spoken by the Elves.

-10-
How many Elves are there?

More than enough to accomplish all that Santa deems necessary plus one hundred extra—just in case.

-11-
What are the Elves' names?

There is an Elf who shares the name of every boy or girl throughout the world.

Should clever parents try to fool Santa and invent a new name, a new Elf magically appears.

To keep from confusing those Elves with the more numerous popular names and to assure each Elf of their own individuality, Santa repeats the first letter of the Elf's name as many times as is needed to create a new Elf name.

For example, one of the Elves sharing the name Robert *(a very popular and likable name)* is known to Santa as RRRRRRRRRRRRRRRRRRRRR RRRRRRRRRRRRRRRRRRRRRRRRRRRRRRRRRR RRRRRRRRRRRRRRRRRRRRRRRRRRRRRRRRRR RRRRRRRRRRRRRRRRRRRRRRRRRRRRRRRRRR RRRRRRRRRRRRRRRRRRRRRRRRRRRRRRRRRR RRRRRRRRRRRRRRRRRRRRRRRRRRRRRRRRRR RRRRRRRRRRRRRRRRRRRRRRRRRRRRRRRRRR RRRRRRRRRRRRRRRRRRRRRRRRRRRRRRRRRR RRRRRRRRRRRRRRRRRRRRRRRRRRRRRRRRRR RRRRRRRRRRRRRRRRRRRRRRRRRRRRRRRRRR RRRRRRRRRRRRRRRRRRRRRRRRRRRRRRRRRR RRRRRRRRRRRRRRRRRRRRRRRRRRRRRRRRRR RRRRRRRRRRRRRRRRRRRRRRRRRRRRRRRRRR RRRRRRRRRRRRRRRRRRRRRRRRRRRRRRRRRR RRRRRRRRRRRRRRRRRRRobert.

His friends prefer to call him Bob.

-12-
What's Santa's favorite food?

As a citizen of the world, Santa enjoys each and every one of the world's different cuisines. He particularly likes to try different spices and seasonings. He loves fruits and vegetables and is a connoisseur of ice cream and other frozen desserts.

-13-
Is there any food Santa doesn't eat?

Venison.

-14-
How much does Santa weigh?

This is a closely guarded secret that Santa and Mrs. Claus try to keep from the Reindeer.

Suffice it to say that Santa's weight, which he prefers to express in terms of Christmas tree ornaments, would decorate all the Christmas trees in five of the world's countries and seven states in the United States.

-15-
What are the Elves' jobs?

Every Elf can do, and does, every job at the North Pole. Not only does this cross-training make for more efficient operations, but it also gives each Elf a chance to show off "multipole" talents.

All the jobs at the Pole are arranged by Christmas categories.

Some of the categories are: Toy Making, Correct Address and Bedtime Analysis, Reindeer Washing, Candy Cane Painting, Good Little Boy and Girl Reporting, Christmas Tree Counting and Inspection, Snowflake Counting and Inspection, List Making, Sleigh Maintenance and Polishing, List Checking, and List Double-Checking.

-16-
Are the Elves boys or girls?

Sorry. There are neither boy nor girl Elves. All Elves share one singular, gentle gender. It's ELF* *(from which they take their name)*.

Although, at first sight, their physical appearance may bear a slight resemblance to either the male or female of the human species, to the Elves themselves these differences are no more important than the color of your socks or size of your hat.

A little-known Elf fact is that the color of their hair, which ranges from the darkest through the lightest shades among all the world's population, changes on a weekly basis. These hair color changes also include the more traditional Elf shades of orange, green, and purple.

*Extra-Lovable Friend

-17-
What's Santa's favorite kind of music?

Christmas Music, closely followed by Rock and Roll, Classical, Folk, Country, Rhythm and Blues, Jazz, Contemporary, and last, but not least, New Age Elf.

-18-
Do the Elves ever misbehave?

No, the Elves are, and always have been, on extraordinarily good behavior.

They do have a rather unusual sense of humor and have a habit of playing jokes and tricks on one another. *(Like the year they painted white and red stripes on the candy canes instead of the required red and white ones.)*

The Elves like to think of themselves as the original "Wild Bunch." Two of the "rascaliest" of the group are named Jackie and Christine.

-19-
Does Santa have any brothers or sisters?

Neither Santa nor Mrs. Claus has any brothers or sisters.

This circumstance has never ever made either of them lonely, as their many, many "Helpers" *(who look remarkably like them and appear all over at Christmas time)*, more than make up for that.

When you take into account the "uncount-able" Elves, the love of all the world's children, and the friendship of all its adults...what more family could Santa and Mrs. Claus ask for?

-20-
How old are the Elves?

Santa finds it easier to explain the age of an Elf in terms of Christmas Music.

Simply put, an Elf's age, at any moment, is a multiple of the times that someone has sung, played, or listened to that particular Elf's favorite Christmas song.

The youngest of the Elves may be only 1,000 songs old, while the oldest can easily be well over 100 million!

-21-
What is Santa's favorite Christmas Eve snack?

The answer to this question is an altogether too well-known "secret," according to Mrs. Claus. It's milk and cookies *(any kind will do, but chocolate is most appreciated).*

-22-
What's Rudolph The Red-Nosed Reindeer's middle name?

The.

-23-
What kind of treats do the Reindeer like?

On Christmas Eve the Reindeer* appreciate any kind of crunchy vegetable. Celery, carrots, radishes, and lettuce are all amongst their favorites. A little vegetable dip or peanut butter to go with the munchies is always appreciated. An occasional sugar cube or candy won't be turned down either!

* Rudolph's favorite treat is bubble gum. He's not allowed to chew it while airborne *(too much risk of popping a bubble over his nose and shutting down Santa's navigational system)*.

-24-

How does Santa visit the whole world in one night?

This is possibly the second most frequently asked question about Santa. Again, the answer may surprise you.

Almost everybody thinks about how *fast* Santa must have to work to accomplish as much as he does in one evening. Focusing on speed is a big mistake and it's where most Yuletide logic takes a wrong turn. Santa accomplishes his work in just the opposite manner!

He has the unique ability to stop time wherever he may be at the moment.

This allows him to travel from place to place at a speed of his own choosing, to remain there for as long as is necessary to accomplish his tasks, and to leave without having perceptibly disturbed time as mortals might measure it.

Many people have come closer to the truth than they knew when saying, "Santa does his work in the blinking of an eye." Although to Santa it's much more leisurely than that.

You already know *(or are able to calculate)* how fast Santa and his Reindeer can travel. Now, you know how he visits the whole world in one night.

With that knowledge, you probably won't be surprised to learn that he's never even come close to being late for the special breakfast Mrs. Claus cooks for him and the Elves each Christmas morning.

-25-
What if there's no snow where Santa visits?

No snow is no problem to Santa. Not only is it a perfectly acceptable climatic condition, but in some places a contrary situation would be quite extraordinary. *(Hawaii, Africa, and South America!)*

Santa explains that "North Pole snow," because of its distance from the Equator, and the lessened gravitational pull, is lighter, fluffier, smoother, whiter, slipperier, and stickier than ordinary snow *(sometimes found elsewhere in the world)*. As a result, the quality and quantity of the snow that sticks to the runners of Santa's sleigh as it leaves the Pole is more than enough to assure smooth sledding on Christmas Eve, as Santa travels to the world's snowiest and snow-less places.

-26-
How does Santa get all the toys into the sleigh at one time?

When one considers that the toys and presents delivered by Santa take up, on average, approximately 12 billion cubic feet *(give or take a medium-sized Christmas ornament)*, it's amazing how they all fit into the sleigh.

The truth of the matter is that the sleigh has nothing to do with it.

It's the magic of "Santa's Sack," into which all of the Christmas toys and presents always fit *(with a little room left over for some special surprises)*, that does the trick. Even Santa's not sure how the sack works, but its magic has never failed him yet.

-27-
How does Santa get up or down a chimney?

Santa needs only to inhale cold air or exhale warm air (*notice he didn't say* "hot air") to control his direction of travel. Standing atop your roof and inhaling some cool night air zips him down the chimney. Placing a finger to the side of his nose and exhaling some warm air changes his body weight and propels him "roofwards."

Except for an occasional sooty smudge, this tried and true system has worked without fail for Santa ever since he began his annual Christmas Eve visits.

(Please, don't try this at home by yourself. Remember, Santa is a professional; without proper training, you might lose control and end up clogging the flue.)

-28-
What if a home has no chimney?

To tell the truth, Santa uses chimneys only because of their convenience when parking his sleigh on a roof.

He's never been reluctant to use other methods of entering a home, provided they meet his one additional requirement. His entryway, be it a door, portal, or window, must also be able to admit both moonlight and starlight.

As there isn't a home anywhere in the world that doesn't meet that specification, Santa's means of entry, while it varies from home to home, is always assured.

-29-
What if there's a fire burning in the fireplace?

Ooops! You forgot the answer to Question 24.

Where Santa stops on Christmas Eve, time stops. That also includes the time it takes for a flame or a spark to rise.

A fire burning in a fireplace is no problem to Santa.

In fact, he frequently comments on how attractive the colors of the flames are as they're momentarily stopped in time. He finds them as uniquely beautiful as the personalities of the people whose homes they warm.

-30-
Does Santa have a telephone?

Yes, he does. The area code is very, very, very long, and the number even longer *(due to the great distance the North Pole is from everyplace else on earth).*

To help him remember the number, Santa gave one part of it on a sheet of paper to each of the Elves. Some Elf sneezed. The sneeze wasn't your garden-variety, wimpy, inconspicuous, not-to-be worthy-of-notation-or-recordation sneeze. Rather, it was a humongous, wide-screen, deserves-its-own-place-in-the-history-books, true "North Pole beauty." It blew the paper sheets out of each of the other Elves' hands and scattered them all over. To this day the Elves still haven't been able to reconstruct the correct number.

When they do, Santa has promised to publish the number throughout the world, and you'll be able to call him "pole-free."

-31-
Which Elf sneezed?

No one's quite sure which Elf sneezed.

Rumor has it that the particular Elf's name began with an "R."

-32-
Is Santa ever sad?

Santa is perpetually jolly and constantly in the best of humor. All this comes naturally to him, and it requires no effort on his part whatsoever. It's in his DNA—December Nice Attitude.

There are conflicting reports from certain Elves, who were present when Santa learned of some little boy's or girl's unpleasant behavior or discourtesy, and heard him make a sound resembling a quiet sniffle. As such Santa sounds have never been officially documented, the accuracy of these reports is left to the reader.

-33-
What kind of sleigh does Santa use?

Santa's sleigh is very, very, very special. In fact, it's the only one of its kind in the whole world.

It's made of the strongest, lightest, smoothest, softest, and most beautiful wood from each of the seven continents. It's as strong as can be and lighter than a feather.

The paint is 10,000 coats deep and so shiny that you can see your own reflection in it at a distance of 1,000 candy canes.

The seats are stuffed with the fluffiest white clouds you've ever seen and are so soft and warm that one could travel forever without becoming tired or chilled.

The open cockpit allows for an unobstructed view of the whole sky and makes it much easier for the Reindeer to hear Santa's commands, which, because Santa's extremely courteous, are more in the nature of polite requests.

The instrument panel, which would be the envy of any modern airplane pilot, has all the special instruments Santa needs to keep him on course, on time, and on the way to you.

The runners and metal fittings are of pure gold with silver trim, polished to reflect the moonlight and starlight that helps to illuminate Santa's path through the skies.

Gold pin-striping on all of the sides and a big brass "SC" monogram on the front complete the detailing.

Should you ever be fortunate enough to see Santa's sleigh, you'll recognize it at once—and never forget it.

-34-

Does Santa have a lot of money?

Santa has no money and no use for it. Everything he needs or wants is available to him, in more than sufficient supply, at the North Pole.

Besides, Santa is in the business of giving and money usually involves selling.

Santa knows that the love and caring he shares with all who believe in him, and in what he represents, is more valuable than all the gold, silver, diamonds, emeralds, and cereal box tops in the world.

In this way Santa knows he is wealthier than a hundred jillion gazillionaires...put together.

-35-
Does Santa have any children?

Santa considers all who believe in him, regardless of their age, to be his children.

-36-
Does Santa have any pets?

Nine of his closest business associates are his "pets."

-37-
Will Santa know if I've moved since he last visited me?

Santa assigns a rather large number of Elves to updating and keeping track of where he'll be making his Christmas Eve stops.

While this used to be a much more time-consuming effort, the use of computers has made it a lot easier.

So, if you've moved since last Christmas, rest assured Santa knows where you live. Even if you're "just visiting" when he makes his rounds, he'll still know where to leave your presents.

Remember, over all the years Santa's been delivering presents, he's never missed bringing the right present to the right person at the right place. Right?

Does Santa really read the letters he gets?

Santa absotively, posolutely, and most assuredly reads each and every letter sent to him.

What's more, as he reads them he assigns an Elf to processing the letter. This is a double check to make sure that all unusual requests, special instructions, and other important information needed by Santa or the Elves, is accurately and properly recorded.

Because Santa and the Elves read very, very fast, the large number of letters he receives is not a problem for him. However, he has commented that, over the last several centuries, the writing seems to be getting smaller.

-39-
Will Santa always bring what I ask for?

The difference between what someone asks for and what they really need is something only one as wise in the ways of the world as Santa would know.

If you ask Santa for a particular present, he'll try his best to respond to you. Should you not receive exactly what you asked for, don't be disappointed. Rather, be assured that Santa always has a very special reason why he thought it best to answer your request in another way.

In time, you'll understand the reason why, and you'll know that Santa's decision was made with the special love and caring he reserves for each of those who believe in him.

-40-
Who wraps the presents Santa brings?

Surprising as it may seem, Santa relies primarily on the Reindeer to wrap the presents he brings. Of course, every year a number of the Elves succeed in bribing the Reindeer with treats, and end up getting to help out with the wrapping *(which is one of the funnest jobs at the Pole).*

Two interesting facts about North Pole presents:

1.

"Official" North Pole wrapping paper
is red and green
(Not green and red).

2.

Sometimes, the best presents Santa brings are
not wrapped at all!

-41-
When is Santa's birthday?

Strange as it may seem, neither Santa nor Mrs. Claus has a birthday, as you and I understand the word.

Even if they did, after the first five hundred years or so, who really keeps count? Indeed, who really cares?

To them, each and every day is as special as your birthday is to you. Santa and Mrs. Claus see no reason to limit such special happiness to a single day, when there are 364 always available.

If you insist on sending them a birthday card, Santa and Mrs. Claus suggest that you do it on your birthday. It will be doubly special and mean as much to them as it does to you.

-42-
Where does Santa get his clothes?

If you mean his "Santa Suit," that's made by Mrs. Claus.

If you're asking about his everyday clothes, he gets them at the same places you do. The only difference is that Santa usually shops by mail order because his presence in a store, along with several thousand Elves *(acting as his fashion advisers)*, frequently proves to be too great a distraction to the other customers.

Although they don't generally advertise it, all clothing stores carry a special size, "XLSSS" *(Extra Large Special Santa Size).*

It's highly unlikely that you'll ever come across this particular size label. But if you should, you can be pretty sure that Santa will be shopping there soon.

-43-

How does Santa decide the order in which he makes his Christmas Eve visits?

Santa chooses his route each Christmas Eve according to a very exact set of random rules. The procedure is extremely complex and varies so much from century to century that to explain it completely would take far too long. Besides, it will probably change next year.

But, to give you an idea of how it works, these are a few of the factors that Santa takes into account:

How bright are the stars shining?
Is there a wind blowing from any direction?
How good have the children been?
What time do they go to bed?
Which direction would Santa like to go first?

What is the phase of the moon?
How fast asleep are the children?
How happy is the home?
Which direction would the Reindeer like to go
first?
How much do the children believe in him?
How many presents are to be delivered?
The number of letters in each child's
name;
The number of letters that aren't
in each child's name;
The International Date Line;
The Equator;
The color of the lights on the Christmas tree;
And last but not least,
The size, weight, color, and shape of the
presents to be delivered.

As you can plainly see, the end result of Santa's calculations and considerations may take him first to Australia, then New York City, down to the tip of Argentina, back to Hong Kong, over to Paris, then to Africa, back over to the USA and Cedarburg, WI, etc., etc., etc.

The only important thing about the order of his visits is that he stops for everyone who believes in him and leaves something.

Santa's never missed yet.

-44-
Who takes care of Santa's home and workshop?

Everybody who lives and works at the North Pole helps out around the house and shop. In fact, with all the Christmas work to be done, being asked to help out around the house is a real treat, bordering on a reward. *(That's not much of a surprise. It's probably the same at your house.)*

Elves, Reindeer, snowmen, snow-women, and of course Mr. and Mrs. Claus all take turns at cleaning, painting, and polishing up the place. Yard work, including snow mowing, raking and recycling fallen icicles, and trimming the frost on the trees, are full-time jobs and some of the most sought-after assignments.

Does bad weather make it hard for Santa to drive the sleigh?

Weather is weather to Santa. He doesn't consider any weather bad *(although sometimes he finds it a little "extreme").*

To overcome any climatic disturbance Santa might encounter, the sleigh is equipped with an "**AAAAAAAAAAAAAAAAAAAAAAAAAAA**" *(Adventitiously Advanced Automatic Arithmetically Articulated Analog Antimass Altitude Adjusting Atmospheric Aura Analyzing Accelerator And Associated Antithetical Amplitude Antimatter Accentuator And Aromatically Augumented And Atomically Accurized Antipasto Assembler).*

This device is similar to the compass on a modern airplane. Cleverly designed to look *(and work)* like a microwave oven, it has an adjustable range of 1,000 to 10,000 candy canes, and assures Santa of a smooth and comfortable trip anywhere he goes in the world.

Unfortunately, the "A-27" still isn't quite perfected and can't completely compensate for the occasional patch of "thought turbulence" generated by unhappy thoughts or unpleasant situations on the ground. The Elves are working on an improved model to fix that, but for now, Santa finds it best to avoid those situations if at all possible, and suggests you do the same.

-46-
Where can I write to Santa?

Letters, cards, notes, or whatever you care to send need only be addressed to:

Santa Claus

C/O North Pole

There isn't a post office, delivery service, express agency, friend, realtive, or parent anywhere in the world who won't see to it that whatever you send gets to Santa.

Are presents exchanged at the North Pole?

Interestingly enough, the practice of exchanging Christmas presents just never seemed to catch on at the North Pole.

Exchanged in mass quantity, however, are hugs.

You can be certain that nothing in the world will bring a tear to your eye or gladden your heart as much as the sight of Reindeer hugging Elves, Elves hugging Reindeer, Reindeer hugging snowmen, snowmen hugging Elves, snowmen hugging Reindeer back, Santa hugging Elves, Mrs. Claus hugging Elves, Mrs. Claus hugging Santa, Elves hugging Santa back, Santa hugging Mrs. Claus back, Reindeer hugging Mrs. Claus, Santa hugging Reindeer, Santa and Reindeer hugging snowmen, snowmen and Mrs. Claus hugging other snowmen, etc., etc., etc.

-48-
What do the Elves like to eat?

Fast Food, Slow Food, Right-Side-Up and Upside-Down Cakes, Chinese Food, Italian Food, Every Other Country Food, Carry-Out Food, Take-In Food, Frozen Food, Fresh Food, Organic Food, Gourmet Food, Special Food, Angel Food, Ordinary Food, Home-Cooked Food, and just about every other kind of food you can think of!*

By the way, the Elves eat between three and thirty-three meals a day, in any order, and at any time!

*Again, excepting venison.

What do the Reindeer do for fun?

They play games, games, and even more games. *(You're probably familiar with that famous song about "Reindeer games.")*

Reindeer are renowned for their game-playing abilities and enthusiasm. *(Did you ever try to play ping-pong against an opponent holding four paddles at one time? You can bet your hoofies it's hard!)* Their list of favorites goes on and on and includes everything from board games to sports. Why, there isn't a game you can think of that they don't like to play.

If you ever get the chance to play with them, try to avoid any winter sports. For some reason, they're really, really, really good at those games.

-50-
Is Santa tired after delivering all the world's presents?

Delivering the entire world's presents is a very, very, very big job.

Because he's been at it so long, Santa makes it look a lot easier than it really is. Fortunately, he's always been able to count on the help of those who believe in him.

It's still tiring work, however, and Santa's been known to take a kitten nap *(which is a little shorter than a cat nap)* after finishing the delicious breakfast Mrs. Claus always has waiting for him when he gets home.

-51-
Why is Santa's suit red?

As you know, the universally recognized Christmas colors are red and green.

When Santa came on the scene, green had been chosen *(by almost every Christmas tree that ever was)*. Red not only looked good on him, it was the only color left.

From what Santa's been able to tell, he made a good choice because nobody's ever complained and he's never been mistaken for a Christmas tree.

-52-
Do any animals besides the Reindeer live at the North Pole?

Many animals make their home at the North Pole. Almost every animal on earth has visited the Pole at one time or another *(usually at the invitation of one of the Reindeer)*.

Perhaps the most unusual animal living at the North Pole *(which is the only place on Earth where it's found)* is a large, long, low, big, floppy-eared, sad-faced, perpetually friendly kind of "dawg." Known as a Hasset Bound *(or by its scientific name: Canis Funnyus Lookingus)*, it's easily recognized by an unusual and singularly distinguishing feature—reindeer-like antlers. Hasset Bounds can travel great distances by gliding with their long wing-like ears fully extended. When they're not practicing sleeping, one or more of them can usually be found keeping close company with Santa.

How cold is it at the North Pole?

The temperature at the Pole is pretty cool, but not as cold as is often reported.

The warmth of the love and respect that all who live and work there have for one another takes just enough of the chill out of the ice and snow to make it more than comfortable.

Santa says the best way to explain North Pole weather is to think of the nicest day you can remember *(from where you live)*, then add snow, ice, Reindeer, and Elves.

That's just how pleasant North Pole weather is—every day!

-54-
Do the Elves ever go with Santa on Christmas Eve?

Sometimes, sometimes not. It all depends upon how busy the schedule is that particular Christmas Eve, as well as the size, shape, and number of the presents to be delivered and whether or not any will require feeding.

Just as in everyday life, circumstances change. The same thing is true for Santa. So, while it's not unusual to have one or more Elves accompanying him on his Christmas Eve travels, many times he's made the trip alone, giving all of the Elves a much deserved night off.

-55-
Does Santa have any hobbies?

The list of Santa's hobbies doesn't seem to have an end. Over the years, Santa's participated in just about every hobby ever invented.

As busy as this century has proven to be, he's had to limit his active participation to no more than several hundred at a time. Amongst his favorite recreational pursuits are music, art, and reading. He's *always* reading.

His favorite kinds of books are History, Travel, and Coloring.

-56-
What sports does Santa like?

Santa's a big sports fan. He enjoys all the world's sporting events, closely follows each and every one *(your school, municipal, and neighborhood teams are amongst his favorites)*, and roots for all who participate. Occasionally he'll attend a public sporting event *(you may even have seen him at one)*, although he usually prefers to take advantage of the perfect reception his home at the top of the world offers, and watch on t-**elf**-a-vision with the rest of us.

Do the Elves ever get to leave the North Pole?

Most certainly and most often. The Elves perform many tasks for Santa away from the North Pole.

You already know that they check on good little boys and girls and report back to Santa. The Elves gladly run all kinds of Elf errands for Santa and Mrs. Claus.

For example, they inspect Christmas trees to see if they're properly decorated. *(When necessary, they leave notes suggesting improvements to the decorations. If you've never received an Elf-O-Gram about your Christmas tree, you should be pleased to know that it was judged as one of the most beautifully decorated ones in the world.)*

-58-
How do I know if a present really came from Santa?

There are lots of ways to tell if a present really came from Santa. Any one of three easy ways will do.

First, if it's what you asked Santa for, there's a pretty good chance that he had something to do with it.

Second, if the paper is red and green *("Official" North Pole wrapping paper colors)*, that's a pretty good indication that it's from your red-suited friend.

And third, if the tag on the present reads "LOVE, Santa"* you can rest assured it's authentic.

North Pole shorthand for:
Labor **O**f **V**arious **E**lves.

-59-
Has anybody ever caught an Elf?

I think you're confusing Elves with leprechauns *(to whom they bear a striking resemblance)*.

More importantly, why would you even want to catch an Elf? In no time at all your home would be filled to overflowing with presents and you'd be forced to move. Not only that, but where there's one Elf there are more, and even if you did move to a bigger home, the additional Elves and presents would have you out of there in no time. Don't forget, you'd have to feed the little people too. And oh boy, do they eat *(re-read Question #48)*!

So, there really isn't much advantage to catching an Elf and you're far better off trapping leprechauns *(who are reported to have gold and wishes in abundant supply)*.

However, if you insist on trying, you'll have to catch your Elf the same way you catch a moonbeam or a loving thought—with your heart.

-60-
What does Santa do about a bad little boy or girl?

This question represents a big misunderstanding about Santa's love for children and all who believe in him.

First, Santa doesn't consider any little boy or girl "bad."

Santa prefers to think of children whose behavior leaves room for improvement as only slightly less than good, or at the very worst, naughty. *("Bad" is a word Santa reserves for certain adults, and fortunately, he's encountered very few deserving of the term over the centuries.)*

Second, Santa finds rewarding the good that's in every little boy or girl a far better way to improve his or her behavior.

Third, the old story about Santa bringing lumps of coal or bags of sticks is no longer ecologically appropriate. *(Besides, that kind of stuff messes up the inside of the sleigh something fierce.)*

-61-
What do Elves wear?

Elf clothes. What else did you expect?

However, just as with snowflakes, no two Elves dress alike. So that when you encounter your next Elf, you won't think them "fashion impaired," remember, Elves consider it very "trendy" to wear colors that clash as well as clothing styles that are mismatched, out of date, and irregularly sized.

In every other respect, their taste in clothes is pretty Elf-ordinary and there's really nothing remarkable about their attire. Except maybe the mystery as to why, even though they wear boots, they leave "footprints" when walking through the snow.

Santa's pretty sure the answer to that mystery's written down somewhere else—perhaps in another book.

What does it look like at the North Pole?

Santa and Mrs. Claus, together with all the other polar citizens, live, work, and play at the North Pole. It's a very large place and to describe it completely would take far too long. To give you an idea of how it's arranged, Santa made the diagram on the next page for you.

1. North Pole *(absolute top and center of the world)*
2. Santa's house *(99 rooms)*
3. Toy shops, present manufacturing, present wrapping, and information *(computer)* center
4. Elf housing and more Elf housing *(the dwelling at 1234 Jingle Bell Boulevard is the original Elf house, and is generally regarded as the oldest building at the North Pole. Listed in the Directory of Hysterical Places, it's easily recognized by its round silver roof. "Locals" refer to it as the "Old Gnome Chrome Dome Home.")*
5. Community Center *(25-screen theatre, 12 indoor hockey rinks, 11 football fields, 10 soccer fields, 9 baseball diamonds, 101-hole golf course, and 21-gazillion-volume library)*
6. "Santaport" with runways for sleigh

7. Swimming pool *(with individually adjustable depth and temperature controls)*
8. Reindeer residence *(never ever referred to as "stables," or worse yet, "barn")*
9. Garage for sleigh *(wash, wax, and polish area)*
10. Christmas tree garden *(perennials only!)*

**Santa's
North Pole**

**Scale of Smiles
1"=10,000 Candy Canes**

-63-
What does Mrs. Claus like to do for fun?

Mrs. Claus has almost as many hobbies and recreational interests as Santa. But if you wanted her to pick out her favorite form of recreation, more likely than not she'd choose ice skating with Santa.

-64-
Does Santa ever get to take a vacation?

He certainly does! As a matter of fact he usually takes several a year. *(He has to; there isn't a hotel or vacation complex anywhere in the world that can accommodate all the Elves at one time, not to mention the Reindeer.)*

One of the biggest advantages Santa enjoys, while travelling the whole world on Christmas Eve, is the opportunity to check out possible vacation spots. He knows them all, including your favorite one. So don't be surprised if you meet him skiing down a mountain, in a hotel lobby, or surfing off a sunny beach. You may not immediately recognize him "out of uniform." However, the several thousand Elves hanging around are usually a pretty good give-away.

-65-
Does Santa ever play with the Christmas toys?

He sure does. In fact, he plays with them all. Stuffed animals, dolls, musical instruments, model trains, and toy soldiers seem to be his special favorites.

Mrs. Claus thinks Santa's the world's "biggest" little boy.

-66-
Do the Elves have any hobbies?

The answer is yes. In fact it's a thousand, no, wait, ten thousand times, yes. But if they had to pick a favorite, it would probably be fotography.

One of them may even have taken a picture of you and Santa when you last visited with him.

They're very good at picture taking. The best picture takers often write e.l.f.* after their names.

expert-like-fotographer

-67-
How does Santa know where he is on Christmas Eve?

Santa holds the original pilot's license. Seriously, ask any airplane pilot you know what Santa's pilot's license number is and they'll tell you it's #1.

As far as being worried about getting lost goes, forget that. Santa has the best navigator in the whole world leading the way with that bright red nose of his.

About the only thing Santa finds confusing is that every so often, over the centuries, people seem to rename a city, get rid of a country, or create a new one altogether.

Santa's never quite understood the need to do this because, to him, it's one world, one people, and one planet.

Where does Santa get his hair cut and beard trimmed?

Santa's never had to travel very far for that. Several of the Elves are barbers and beauticians (*that's why Mrs. C. always looks so pretty*), or "Santa Stylists" *(as they prefer to be called)*.

You probably knew that but just didn't know you did.

The amazing resemblance between the old-fashioned "barber pole" and the "North Pole" didn't just happen by accident, you know.

-69-
Does Santa ever get sick?

Santa, Mrs. Claus, the Elves, the Reindeer, and all the other polar personnel are immune to germs and sickness because of their "Merry Christmas Metabolism."

In addition to that, Mrs. C. always sees to it that everything at the Pole is neat and tidy. You might even say she makes sure it's super Santa-tized.

Except for an occasional allergic sneeze *(usually in response to the extremely infrequent unhappy thought that may make its way up to and over the Pole)*, illness is a word that won't be found in Santa's dictionary.

He always wishes that were true of all the world's dictionaries.

-70-
Does Santa have any other jobs?

Santa thinks that his present Christmas career is far too important to all who believe in him even to think about changing jobs.

However, in his spare time, Santa frequently tries to help people out in any way he can. Although his success rate isn't as high as his present delivery accuracy *(1,000%!)*, it's still good to know that Santa's on your side.

A little-known Santa fact: ships in need of assistance invented a distress signal commonly referred to as "S.O.S."

It stands for **"S**end **O**ut **S**anta!"

How does Santa decide which Elf to take with him when he leaves the North Pole?

Santa makes sure each and every Elf *(as well as all of his other polar pals)* gets to go with him on his travels.

The opportunity to accompany Santa when he visits with children just before Christmas is a very much sought-after Elf privilege. To make the selection fair, and a game, Santa and Mrs. Claus came up with the idea for a contest.

Each day, the Elf who paints the straightest stripes on that day's candy canes wins a trip with Santa. This not only contributes to the overall frivolity at the Pole, but the quality of the candy canes has improved remarkably.

So if you see an Elf with Santa, when he's out visiting before his "big trip," you'll know that Elf's a winner *(in more ways than one)*.

-72-
Why does Santa always say "Ho Ho Ho?"

Surprisingly enough, and even though this phrase is widely associated with Santa, very few people actually know what it means or why he's always repeating it.

"Ho Ho Ho," which is more accurately spelled "H.O. H.O. H.O." *(Santa says the other way's okay too),* is a secret coded instruction to all who believe in Santa *(or all he hopes will come to believe in him)* to "Help Out, Help Out, Help Out." *(Not just at Christmas time, but during the whole year long.)*

Santa says: be sure to share the secret code with a friend.

-73-
How long will Santa exist?

Santa and Mrs. Claus came into existence because of the power of love and caring in the world *(which seems to reach maximum levels at Christmas time)*.

They'll be around as long as one child *(of any age)* believes in them.

And, since nobody is ever too old to have a wonderful childhood, their continued existence, for a long, long, long time, is pretty well assured.

-74-
Is there really a pole at the North Pole?

There most certainly is a pole at the North Pole.

If there wasn't, the whole idea of calling the place "The North Pole" wouldn't make any sense.

The North Pole pole *(which has the first set of red and white stripes ever painted)* is very special. Not only does it serve as the world's most accurate navigational aid, it also radiates love, caring, sharing, concern for others, giving, joy, happiness, and peace to the rest of the world.

This might also explain the colors of Santa's suit.

-75-
What does "New Age Elf" music sound like?

As reported elsewhere in this book, New Age Elf is one of Santa's favorite kinds of music.

It sounds much like early Rock and Roll. In fact, there are many who believe that Rock and Roll music was derived from New Age Elf. That probably has something to do with the story about a certain little boy who asked for a guitar for Christmas and the Elf assigned to processing his request.

Legend has it that the particular gnome's name was "ELFIS"... and the rest is history.

Are there any cats at the North Pole?

If you're looking to find the more common breeds of cats *(Persian, Siamese, and Heinz 57)*, you won't find them *(or any of their relatives)* at the North Pole. What you will find is a kind of obnoxiously friendly feline known as a Christmas Cat. Found only at the Pole, it differs from its southern relations only slightly, mainly in that:

1. Christmas Cats have tails 10-20 times longer than those of ordinary cats, which they use to block the drafts of cold air that come in under doors.

2. Christmas Cats constantly wish everyone a "Meowy Christmas."

3. Christmas Cats have either solid or striped coats. The solid colors vary amongst those found on Christmas tree lights and the stripes are the color of Christmas ribbons *(red and green being the most common)*.

-77-

Is there a newspaper at the North Pole?

You bet your Christmas cookies there is!

In fact there's a morning and an evening paper. One is the "Polar Press" and the other is the "North Pole News."

Both publish only joyful and good news, which frequently requires special editions and daily supplements. The most popular section in each of the papers is always the Elf employment ads *(which list that day's most fun jobs).*

Interestingly enough, both papers are edited by one very busy and talented Elf, named Christmas Chris. All the other Elves H.O. H.O. H.O. *(Help Out, Help Out, Help Out)* as her reporters.

-78-
Does Santa ever get angry?

Santa's personality has no room for anger, which is absolutely contrary to his character.

About as close to "angry" as Santa has been known to get is "perturbed." And that's happened only when he's had to check the dictionary at your local library to find out if the words "war," "poverty," "disease," and "sadness" are still in it.

Santa would really appreciate it if you could work with him to help get rid of those words.

-79-
Can Santa stop bad things from happening?

Oh my, how often Santa has wished he could do that!

However, that kind of ability is reserved for a much higher Power.

Santa's abilities, although quite broad, are still limited. He mainly concerns himself with trying to help make good things happen. His traditional efforts are stored in your memory, along with his special efforts, which are stored in your heart.

-80-
What time zone is the North Pole in?

You're certainly aware of the fact that each time zone, throughout the world, is next to another. Because the world is as round as a Christmas tree ornament, the tips of the time zones all touch at one place. And, even though you may never have realized it, it's at the North Pole that they all come together.

This means that whatever time it is, any-where in the world *(including right where you are at this moment)*, it's also the same time at the North Pole. This makes setting Santa's Christmas clock a lot easier. *(Sundials are still a problem, though.)*

-81-
Does Santa drive a car?

He sure does, and he's a very careful and considerate driver.

Since there are normally several thousand Elves around *(universally recognized as the worst "back seat drivers" in the world)*, he generally lets Mrs. C. do the driving.

T
HE
ELVES
WISHU
AMERRY
CHRISTMAS

-82-

Why does Santa wear glasses?

Fine print.

-83-

Does anyone ever get hurt at the North Pole?

Even if everyone at the Pole were not as careful as they are, there's just too much fun in the air to allow for a much more serious injury than a sprained funny-bone *(from laughing too hard)*.

About the closest thing to an injury that Santa can think of is the occasional broken snowman *(which usually happens while they're playing Frosty Football)*. Such situations are never serious. There are always plenty of spare snowman parts sprinkled all over the ground.

-84-
Do the Reindeer have any animal friends?

The Reindeer are amongst the most friendly animals ever to exist and they get along with every other animal, great and small, furry or feathered, wild or domestic, stuffed or unstuffed. Santa's not sure whether they have any animal "best friends," although he's noticed that they do seem to pal around a lot with the snow gnus *(which closely resemble the gnus you've probably seen at your local zoo).*

That may also explain why Blitzen's always going around saying "snow gnus is good gnus."

-85-
What's Santa always writing down?

Lists. Santa's the world's foremost list maker. He keeps them in quadruplicate and numerically alphabetizes them. He has good little boy and girl lists, present lists, grocery lists, lists of names, lists of places, lists of things to do, and just about every other kind of list that you can think of. His longest list is his list of lists list.

-86-
Are the Elves very intelligent?

Elves are super-smart and extremely intelligent. That's probably because Santa's always talking about how valuable a gift knowledge is, and how everyone should try to get the best education they can. In fact the Elves represent every profession, trade, vocation, and employment skill that requires education or training.

All Elves, as soon as they get their names, are awarded a B.S. *(Basic Santa)* degree with a major in "Double E" *(Elementary Elfing)* and a minor in Elfonomics. Many take Santa's advice and continue their education, going on to graduate school and earning their P.H.D. *(Profound Happiness Dispenser)*.

-87-
Can Santa see through walls?

You may be confusing Santa's abilities with those of another adult male *(whose name also begins with an "S")*. But, as long as you asked, the amazing truth is that he can!

Several years ago Santa realized the advantages of being able to see through walls and invented a device to perform that task. He calls it a window.

-88-
Where does Santa get the books he reads?

The North Pole Library is one of Santa's favorite places. It's filled with books that are filled with words, which are filled with knowledge. Many have pictures too.

The North Pole Library contains an original edition of each of the very best books ever written, and has at least one copy for every Elf at the Pole *(that's so no Elf is ever disappointed if they want to borrow a particular book)*.

Obviously, running the library is a pretty big and important job. Santa entrusts the operation of the library to ELF *(meaning, in this case, Extremely Literate Friend)* Lois the Librarian. Because Lois is so very knowledgeable about books, Lois always has tons of spare time to write a weekly book review for each of the polar papers.

-89-
Do the Elves ever sleep?

Sure they do! Elves get tired and need their rest just like you. The only difference is that Elves need very little sleep. Two or three pleasant dreams are generally all that's needed to refresh them completely.

Legend has it that one Elf, Rip Van Elf, slept for forty dreams. Most Elves don't believe that story, and Rip has never admitted to it either.

-90-
What does Santa like to drink?

Only one thing—liquids.

But seriously, Santa drinks many kinds of beverages both for his enjoyment and because they're good for him. He's even been known to take a nip of Christmas Sherry.

-91-
Do the Elves have to go to school?

Elves don't have to go to school—they want to go!

If there's one thing an Elf knows for sure, it's the value of a good education.

They go to USC *(University of Santa Claus)*, Yule, Present State, and Christmas College *(only after receiving their Elementary Elf degree)*. Night school classes are held at Christmas Eve College.

Class work is graded on a scale of "A" through "F."

A = Amazing!	B = Beautiful!
C = Christmas!	D = Delightful!
E = Excellent!	F = Fantastic!

-92-
Do any insects live at the North Pole?

Only one kind of insect lives at the North Pole.

Its natural coloring is that of a beautifully decorated Christmas tree. It has the merriest of dispositions, attributable, no doubt, to its musical inclinations.

These Big And Happy (BAH) insects delight all who live and work at the Pole, as they constantly zip through the air humming Christmas carols.

You'll know one's near the next time you hear someone exclaim "Bah! Humbug."

-93-

Where does Santa get all the batteries for the Christmas presents?

ABE* provide all he needs.

Amazing Battery Elves

-94-
Why are bells always ringing at the Pole?

Actually, what you probably heard were the Christmas cattle talking to each other. Their musical voices are frequently mistaken for bells ringing. Many people sing about them. You know the song, it's called "Jingle Bulls."

-95-
Why don't some people believe in Santa Claus?

This question bothers Santa about as much as anything can. It's not that there aren't enough true believers, it's just that those who don't believe miss out on so much.

Sad to say, there are several unfortunate reasons why some people don't believe in Santa Claus. These reasons are unpleasant, unrealistic, and worst of all, absolutely unnecessary.

Santa knows them as well as he knows his own name, and even keeps track of them that way.

People don't believe in Santa because:
They're too **S**ophisticated,
They suffer from **A** severe case of adulthood,
They claim **N**ot to have enough time,
They **T**hink they're too busy,
They're too "m**A**ture" for their own good,

Also,

They don't have the **C**hristmas spirit,
They need to grow in **L**ove,
They lack im**A**gination,
They don't know how yo**U**thful it will keep them,
Caring and sharing **A**ren't important to them,
They take life far too **S**eriously.

Does Santa have a Christmas tree?

Christmas trees are found in great abundance at the North Pole. The climate allows them to stay fresh all year and they don't need to be taken down.

Santa has a very special tree in his home, which is decorated with pictures of all the Christmas trees people have decorated for this Christmas *(remember, the Elves check on Christmas trees and take pictures)*. He gets the ornaments from Elf NNNNNNancy, who runs the Sugar Plum Shoppe and is very nnnnnice.

Santa recalls that last year, the picture of your tree was on one of the uppermost branches, right next to the star at the top.

-97-
How does Santa find his way home to the North Pole?

That's easy. The brightest star in the sky on Christmas Eve is always the North Star, which is right over the North Pole and Santa's home.

It's easy to find because it's right next to the Big Dipper, which is a very well-known constellation *(sometimes referred to as the Great Bear, or by its scientific name, Ursus Bigus Friendlius Ofus Allus)*.

When he's finished his rounds, all Santa needs to do is point out the North Star to the Reindeer and he's as good as home—safe, sound, and starry-eyed.

"IBIS"
"IBIS"
"IBIS"

-98-
Do any birds live at the North Pole?

Just about every bird that ever was and a few that weren't live at the North Pole. Many of your own backyard birds fly north for the summer and vacation there. Perhaps the most unusual of Santa's feathered friends is the Christmas Ibis. Although small in size, it has the loudest of voices.

It takes its name from its melodious song-like call, "IBIS, IBIS, IBIS."

Of course, this bird's claim to fame as Santa's favorite fowl has nothing whatsoever to do with the fact that "IBIS" stands for "I Believe In Santa."

-99-
Has Santa ever fallen out of his sleigh?

Goodness gracious golly gee, no! He always wears his "Santa Seat Belt" which holds him safely inside, especially on those high-speed turns the Reindeer like to make around tall buildings, radio and TV towers, and the North Star.

Occasionally, an extra present or surprise may fall out of the sleigh and tumble softly and safely to the ground.

Should you be fortunate enough to find one, keep it with Santa's compliments. Curiously enough, it was probably intended for you in the first place.

-100-
Do the Reindeer have any artistic talents?

You bet they do! They're world-renowned for their singing talents and painting abilities.

Their musical accomplishments include the highest note ever sung, longest note ever held, and most unusual note ever heard. Santa considers their efforts quite noteworthy.

Their painting skills, both brush and finger *(or rather, hoof)* are legendary. They paint everything from landscapes to portraits. Park benches are their specialty.

Elf Arthur helps out with the framing, *(making each painting a true work of Art)*. Their most famous work, shown at the top of the page, hangs in the lower lobby broom closet of the Community Center annex.

It's entitled: **"A Black Cat At The Bottom Of A Coal Mine,On A Dark Night, During A Power Failure."**

-101-
Is There Really a Santa Claus?

1. Yes.
2. Perhaps.
3. No, there's not.

These probably are not the answers you expected. But if, as the author intended and Santa instructed, all of the questions in this book must be answered truthfully, they're the only appropriate response.

You see, the world's population can be divided into four kinds of people: 1. Those who believe in Santa, 2. Those who aren't sure if he exists or not, 3. Those who do not believe in him, and 4. Santa's Elves.

If you're in the vast majority *(those who believe in Santa)*—congratulations! Santa and the author hope you enjoyed this book, and that you will put the information in it to good use.

If you're in the group that's "not sure," the fact that you still have an open mind on the subject is cause for selebration *(Santa likes to spell that word with an "S")*. More probably than not, you'll come to believe in Santa; you just need a little more persuasion. Santa has already noted that, and a number of Elves have been assigned to the task of speeding up the process. While you keep your mind open to the idea, prepare your heart to accept the love and joy that believing in Santa brings.

If you don't believe in Santa, please feel free to go about your life's business.

Try not to let the accuracy of the voluminous amount of information in this book dissuade you from your disbelief.

Relax and enjoy the freedom of not being encumbered by those distracting Christmas stories about Santa.

Take comfort in knowing that, by eliminating Santa from appearing on the Christmas cards you send, your selection process has been measurably simplified *(although the assortment of cards from which you can make your choice has been drastically reduced).*

Sleep soundly Christmas Eve, safe and secure in the knowledge that every flashing light in the sky must be some sort of mechanically propelled aircraft and any strange noise in your home *(on the roof or elsewhere)* can be nothing other than an ordinary household sound, not to be attributed to the coming or going of any red-suited friend.

Revel in having attained sufficient wisdom, on the subject of Santa's existence, to dispense with any consideration of the fact that you're never too old to have a wonderful childhood.

Take satisfaction in knowing beforehand the exact contents and origin of every Christmas present that you may receive.

Avoid the use of red and green wrapping paper lest others think your lack of belief in Santa less than sincere *(see Question #40).*

Save the exertion of unnecessary physical energy in smiling as children recite their wondrous conviction in Santa's existence. Indulge yourself in the self-gratifying awareness of their mistaken belief. Forget that children are amongst the most sage and truthful persons you will ever meet on life's journey.

Welcome the opportunity to tolerate benevolently your adult friends who steadfastly acknowledge the existence of Santa. It goes without saying that your gracious acceptance of their seasonal misapprehension is the bedrock upon which your friendship is built.

Lastly, pay no attention to small elfin-like footprints in the snow. They are, no doubt, easily explained.

If you're an Elf, you don't have time to read any more of this book. There's work to be done! Christmas is closer than you think. Wishes and presents are piling up. The Reindeer are playing games. The North Pole needs polishing. Mrs. Claus is cooking......

Santa's waiting.

OUTDEX

(Close To, But Not Quite, An Index)

C

D

112

J

Jobs

J.O.E. see Names

L

Labels

Languages

Leprechauns

Letters

Library

Lists

Location

Lost

L.O.V.E.

O

P

Q

R

Reindeer

Rudolph

S

Sack

Sad

Santa

T

Other Books From Blue Sky Marketing Inc.

Reflections Of A Small Town Santa, by Bob Litak.
The wonderful story of how trading a briefcase for a Santa sack forever changed the authors life. Soon to be a classic.
Hardcover, 96 pages; 5x7, ISBN: 0-911493-22-0

The Home Owner's Journal: What I Did & When I Did It, by Colleen Jenkins.
The best-selling, easiest-to-use home record keeping book on the market.
Softcover (spiral binding), 136 pages, 6x9, ISBN: 0-911493-11-5

31 Days to RUIN Your Relationship, by Tricia Seymour & Rusty Barrier.
Tongue-in -cheek (reverse psychology) book of laugh-out-loud "affirmations."
Softcover, 80 pages, 6x4, ISBN: 0-911493-21-2

31 Days to INCREASE Your Stress, by Tricia Seymour.
Tongue-in -cheek (reverse psychology) book of laugh-out-loud "affirmations."
Softcover, 80 pages, 6x4, ISBN: 0-911493-19-0

It's So Cold In Minnesota..., by Bonnie Stewart & Cathy McGlynn.

Hilarious, best-selling regional book poking fun at Minnesota winters.

Softcover, 6x4, 96 pages, ISBN: 0-911493-18-2

It's So Cold In Wisconsin..., by Bonnie Stewart & Cathy McGlynn.

Hilarious, new regional book poking fun at Wisconsin winters.

Softcover, 6x4, 96 pages, ISBN: 0-911493-20-4

Vacation Getaway: A Journal for Your Travel Memories.

With 15 pocket pages, it's the best-designed, best valued travel journal on the market.

Softcover (wire spiral binding), 36 pages (including pockets), 5x9, ISBN: 0-9633573-0-1

The Family Memory Book: Highlights of Our Times Together, by Judy Lawrence.

Easy-to-use, fill-in-the-blank book for recording high-lights of family celebrations & holidays.

Hardcover, 96 pages, 7x10, ISBN: 0-911493-13-1

Our Family Memories: Highlights of Our Times Together, by Judy Lawrence.

Leather-like, embossed version of Family Memory Book.

Hardcover, 96 pages, 7x10, ISBN: 0-911493-14-X

Money & Time-Saving Household Hints, from The Leader-Post Carrier Foundation.

Over 1,000 clever, useful, and sometimes startling solutions to everyday problems.

Softcover, 128 pages, 6x9, ISBN: 0-911493-15-8

Other Books From Blue Sky Marketing Inc.
Continued

The Weekly Menu Planner & Shopping List.
The simple and easy way to plan your meals and shopping.
52 weekly sheets, 8.5x11, ISBN: 0-911493-05-0

The Bridal Shower Journal.
Keepsake for recording shower gifts & memories. Includes 25 Thank You cards & envelopes.
Sturdy softcover with spiral wire binding, 22 pages (including 6 pockets), 7x10, ISBN: 0-9633573-2-8

Our Honeymoon: A Journal of Romantic Memories.
With 15 pocket pages, it's the best-designed, best valued honeymoon journal on the market.
Softcover (plastic comb binding), 36 pages (including pockets), 5x9, ISBN: 0-9633573-1-X